ALBERT EINSTEIN

DISCOVER THE LIFE OF AN INVENTOR

Don McLeese

Rourke Publishing LLC
Vero Beach, Florida 32964

© 2006 Rourke Publishing LLC

www.rourkepublishing.com

PHOTO CREDITS: Cover, pgs 8, 10, 18 ©Getty Images; pg 13 ©AFP/Getty Images; Title, pgs 4, 15, ©AIP/Emilio Segre Visual Archives; pgs 7, 16, 21, from the Library of Congress

Title page: *Albert Einstein and his wife, Elsa.*

Library of Congress Cataloging-in-Publication Data

McLeese, Don.
  Albert Einstein / Don McLeese.
    p. cm. -- (Discover the life of an inventor II)
  Includes bibliographical references and index.
  ISBN 1-59515-433-7
  1. Einstein, Albert, 1879-1955--Juvenile literature. 2.
Physicists--Biography--Juvenile literature. I. Title.
  QC16.E5M366 2006
  530'.092--dc22

                              2005011433
Printed in the USA

Rourke Publishing
1-800-394-7055
www.rourkepublishing.com
sales@rourkepublishing.com
Post Office Box 3328, Vero Beach, FL 32964

TABLE OF CONTENTS

THE GENIUS

Some people are smarter than just about everyone else. We have a word for such a person. We call him or her a **genius**. There has never been a more famous genius than Albert Einstein.

Einstein was a great **scientist**, but, most of all, he was a great thinker. The way he thought changed the way that all scientists (and all of us!) think about the world.

Albert Einstein was one of the smartest people who ever lived.

A GERMAN BOY

Albert was born on March 14, 1879, in the country of Germany. He was born in the city of Ulm, but when he was a year old, his family moved to the bigger city of Munich. His father was named Hermann, and his mother was named Pauline.

Einstein was born in Ulm.

THE COMPASS

When Albert was five years old, his father showed him a **compass**. No matter which way Albert moved the compass, the needle would always point to the north. Albert was amazed by this.

His father explained that the needle always pointed north because of a force called "magnetism." It was as if the North Pole was a **magnet**, making the needle point in that direction. Albert wondered about this powerful force, something that couldn't be seen. It was just the beginning of Albert's interest in science.

Young Einstein photographed with his sister

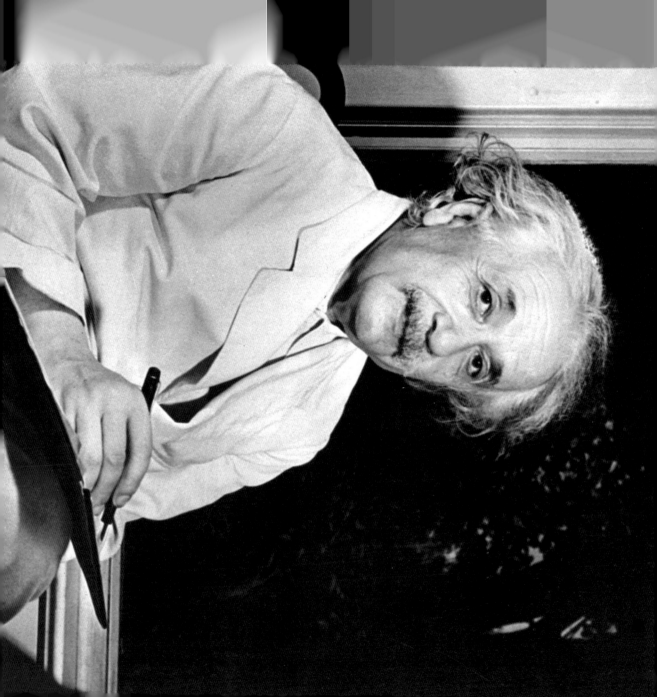

AN AVERAGE STUDENT

Though we now consider Albert one of the smartest people who ever lived, some of his teachers thought he wasn't a very smart boy at all. It took him longer to learn to talk than most children. When he did talk, he had trouble putting his thoughts into words.

As an adult, Einstein was far from average.

Young Einstein also had problems with his memory. He would read things over and over without remembering what he had just read. He was best with numbers, but he sometimes made careless mistakes because he was trying to add or subtract too quickly.

Time *magazine named Einstein "Person of the Century" in 1999.*

DECEMBER 31, 1999 $4.95

TIME

PERSON OF THE CENTURY

ALBERT
EINSTEIN

AN IMPORTANT TEST

When he was 16, Albert took an important test. Those who passed would be allowed to continue their education and become electrical engineers. This was a good job, but Albert failed the test! He continued to study mathematics and science.

Albert Einstein often took time out from his work to enjoy sailing.

IT'S ALL RELATIVE

After graduating from college in 1900, Albert spent much of his time with scientific **experiments**. In 1905, he wrote three papers that changed the scientific field of **physics**. One of these introduced his "special theory of **relativity**."

*A photograph of Einstein
taken in 1947*

Einstein showed how different things relate to each other, such as matter and energy, or time and space. In 1915, he finished a paper that applied his theory to how **gravity** works in the entire universe. He called this his "general theory of relativity."

Einstein demonstrates his theories.   19

PRIZE-WINNING SCIENTIST

In 1922, Albert Einstein was awarded the Nobel Prize in physics. The Nobel Prizes are the most important awards in the world. He moved to the United States in 1933 and lived the rest of his life in Princeton, New Jersey. He continued to work on theories to help explain how the universe worked. When Einstein died on April 18, 1955, he was considered by many the greatest genius who had ever lived.

Einstein became an American citizen in 1940.

IMPORTANT DATES TO REMEMBER

1879   Albert Einstein is born

1884   Albert gets his first compass and becomes very interested in learning how the world works

1900   Albert graduates from college

1905   Albert has a "miracle year" in which he writes three important papers on his theories

1915   Albert writes his "general theory of relativity"

1922   Albert wins the Nobel Prize in physics

1955   Albert Einstein dies

GLOSSARY

compass (KUM pus) — a dial with a needle that points to the north and shows which direction it is

experiments (ek SPARE uh mentz) — tests of something, to try something out

genius (JEE nyus) — a very, very smart person

gravity (GRAV ut ee) — the force of the earth or other large masses that draws smaller things to it.

magnet (MAG net) — an object that draws or attracts other objects to it

physics (FIZ icks) — the science of energy and physical matter

relativity (REL uh TIV ut ee) — how things affect each other or relate to each other

scientist (SI unt ist) — someone who studies nature and how it works

INDEX

Further Reading

Brown, Don. *Odd Boy Out: Young Albert Einstein.* Houghton Mifflin, 2004.
Schaeffer, Lola M. and Wyatt S. *Albert Einstein,* Pebble Books, 2003.

Websites to Visit

www.aip.org/history/einstein/
www.pbs.org/wgbh/nova/einstein/index.html

About the Author

Don McLeese is an associate professor of journalism at the University of Iowa. He has won many awards for his journalism, and his work has appeared in numerous newspapers and magazines. He has written many books for young readers. He lives with his wife and two daughters in West Des Moines, Iowa.